# THE LIGHT OF LOST SUNS

## THE PERSEA SERIES OF POETRY IN TRANSLATION
Daniel Weissbort, *General Editor*

THINGS I DIDN'T KNOW I LOVED:
*Selected Poems of Nazim Hikmet*
Translated by Randy Blasing and Mutlu Konuk

NAZIM HIKMET: THE EPIC OF SHEIK BEDREDDIN
*and Other Poems*
Translated by Randy Blasing and Mutlu Konuk

OSIP MANDELSTAM: 50 POEMS
Translated by Bernard Meares
Introductory essay by Joseph Brodsky

JÁNOS PILINSZKY: SELECTED POEMS
Translated by János Csokits and Ted Hughes
Introduction by Ted Hughes

VASKO POPA: COLLECTED POEMS
Translated by Anne Pennington
Introduction by Ted Hughes

# The Light of Lost Suns

## Selected Poems of Amir Gilboa

Selected and translated
from the Hebrew
*by*
Shirley Kaufman
*with*
Shlomith Rimmon

PERSEA BOOKS / New York

These poems first appeared in Hebrew in the following volumes: *K'hulim Veadumim* (Am Oved Publishers, Ltd., 1963), *Ratsiti Lihtov Siftei Yeshenim* (Hakibbutz Hameuchad Publishing House, Ltd., 1963), *Ayala Eshlah Otah* (Hakibbutz Hameuchad Publishing House, Ltd., 1972).

Copyright © 1979, by Shirley Kaufman
All rights reserved.
For information, address the publisher:
Persea Books, Inc.
225 Lafayette Street
New York, New York 10012

International Standard Book Number: 0-89255-037-6, cloth
0-89255-038-4, paper

Library of Congress Card Catalog Number: 79-88577

First Edition

Printed in the United States of America

## CONTENTS

| | | |
|---|---|---|
| Translator's Acknowledgments | | 9 |
| Introduction | | 11 |

I. from *Blue and Red, Collected Poems* (1946-1963)
- Song of Blue and Red — 23
- Birth — 24
- In the Dark — 25
- Isaac — 26
- Moses — 27
- All Ordinary Things — 28
- Everywhere — 29
- A Red Coral — 30
- Happiness — 32
- If I Had a Hundred Hats — 33
- Our Eyes Closing — 34
- Song All Day Long — 35
- The Kingdom of Silence — 36
- Joshua's Face — 38
- Samson — 39
- In Very Ancient Days — 40

II. from *The Lips of Those Asleep* (1966-1968)
- With Force I'll Seize the End of a Dream — 43
- Every Time I Discover a New America — 44
- What For — 45
- And All This? — 46
- I Go on Disappearing from Myself — 47
- Now Seeing There's Rain — 48
- Those Were the Last Dances — 49

| | | |
|---|---|---|
| | Those Who Know What's in Heaven | 50 |
| | I Know I Won't Come this Way Again | 51 |
| | To Jerusalem My City | 52 |
| | | |
| III. | from *Gazelle, I'll Send You* (1971-1972) | |
| | Gazelle, I'll Send You | 57 |
| | The Whole Land Is Mine | 58 |
| | They Will All Rise | 59 |
| | I Looked Outside | 60 |
| | Far Far Outside | 61 |
| | To Pluck Stars | 62 |
| | The Time of Waking | 63 |
| | A Patch of the Sea | 64 |
| | In the Haze the Sun | 65 |
| | See an Unwalled City | 66 |
| | What Peace for His Soul | 67 |
| | My Secret, Mine, Sees My Face | 68 |
| | Its Leaves Seen | 69 |
| | Squeezed in a Bus | 70 |
| | Standing on Tiptoe | 71 |
| | And on the Great Waters | 72 |
| | Finally I Go to the Man Who Set Traps | 73 |
| | How Would I Stand Then | 74 |
| | All the Time to Sit Here | 75 |
| | How They Run into the Day | 76 |
| | Suddenly with Force | 77 |
| | A Bouquet—To Scatter Its Flowers | 78 |
| | If in Pain a Light Feather | 79 |
| | What Do I Forget | 80 |
| | I'm Certain I Went | 81 |
| | To Move on Slowly Slowly | 82 |
| | Look at this Man | 83 |

IV. from *Recognition Burning* (1974)
    If You Get up and Leave      87
    He'll Take You with Him      88

TRANSLATOR'S ACKNOWLEDGMENTS

Some of these translations have already appeared in *Ariel, Contemporary Literature in Translation, Midstream, Modern Hebrew Literature, Tri-Quarterly, The Webster Review,* and in the following anthologies: *Contemporary Israeli Literature,* The Jewish Publication Society of America (Philadelphia, 1977); *New Writing in Israel,* Schocken Books (New York, 1976); and *New Writing from Israel,* Corgi Books (London, 1976).

I am grateful to Shlomith Rimmon of the Hebrew University in Jerusalem, whose work with me made these translations possible, and to Rivka Maoz, also of the Hebrew University, whose assistance with most of these poems was invaluable for understanding and translating them.

For his close reading of the translations and discerning suggestions, I want to thank my husband, Hillel Daleski, Hebrew University.

I especially appreciate the cooperation of Amir Gilboa himself who met and consulted with me throughout the translation of these poems.

S. K.<br>
*Jerusalem,* 1979

# INTRODUCTION

The poems of Amir Gilboa both celebrate and mourn "the light of lost suns." In an early poem, he wrote, "In very ancient days/everything was sun," but that was before life began on this planet, "a legend born into sadness." Whatever hope there is for man's survival, in a world which has become increasingly complex and terrifying and in which Gilboa feels more and more isolated, lies in man's unconscious memory, his intuitive and chthonic awareness of the archetypal light. This light comes from a sun that goes "straight to [the] head" ("If I Had a Hundred Hats") with the innocent exhilaration of childhood, the poet-child waving and tossing a hundred hats in a hundred colors.

It is no accident, then, that dreams, real and imagined, personal and collective, by night and by day, play such an important part in the poetry of Gilboa. Dreams reveal memory. To wake *from* a dream is to forget. To wake *in* a dream is to arrive at one's source, to recover the light. Prophets and children do this more easily than others. They know what's in heaven, they can recall a miracle. And the prophet and child in Gilboa "dream visions/and hear words in the deep cellars they carry with them" ("Those Who Know What's in Heaven").

There are also moments outside the dream when the poet, neither prophet nor child, feels he is in touch with the universe as it was before man spoiled it. But we are never closer to that first, primeval light, to that ecstasy of awareness, than in the moment when we are born or reborn. Gilboa feels this ecstasy in the freshness of his land after rain: "Oh Lord, how close we've been!" ("Birth"), and expresses it in poems about the rebirth of his nation.

Like many leading Israeli poets, Gilboa has a most intimate relationship with traditional Hebrew literature, starting with the Bible and Talmudic legends, as well as the ability to transcend and compress time so that past and present are one, to connect his personal life to the life of a people.

In a poem like "Isaac," time dissolves as the child and father move through the woods with blood "already on the leaves," and the ancient story of God's challenge to the faith of Abraham is subsumed in the twentieth century destruction of European Jewry. Its title immediately evokes the Biblical story so that we are wary when the poem seems to begin simply as a pleasant tale told by a child. The word translated as "father" (*avi* in Genesis 22) is *abba* in Gilboa's poem, which is really the equivalent of "daddy;" the word for "trees" in Hebrew, *etzim,* also means "wood" (for the burnt offering of the Genesis story). So that throughout the poem we have a child's innocent voice speaking against the Genesis narrative until the poet becomes Isaac, and the father is Abraham as well as the poet's own father. Then in a terrifying reversal of roles, of time and of place, it is the father who is butchered—not on Moriah, where the child might have been sacrificed—but in the forests of Europe, massacred by the Nazis. Gilboa combines the contemporary Holocaust with the Biblical narrative, filtering one through the other until what remains is pure nightmare: "I tore my eyes open/and woke." But his bloodless hand is also the victim's hand, the nightmare pursues him even by day.

Gilboa has been hailed as the voice of his generation. Expressing, as has been suggested, historical continuity with the Biblical tradition, while at the same time experimenting with style, he has been recognized as an iconoclast who broke with the giants of the revival of Hebrew poetry—Bialik, and then Shlonsky and Alterman—to forge his own new poetic diction, rejecting Russian Futurism and Symbolism which influenced the earlier poets. But the tension inherent in adapting an ancient language with its mythic and historic associations to the speech of our time is always evident in his work and poses a special challenge to the translator. This problem is more apparent in Gilboa, especially in his later work, than in most other poets writing in Hebrew today. The meaning of a Gilboa poem emerges as much from the sound-patterns of internal rhymes and alliteration, which are also associative, as directly from the ideas and images. It is almost impossible to render into English his fragmented thought, unusual word relationships, the ways in which a line works backward and forward at the same time (more complex than double meaning), the enjambment, the silences, the leaps. Choices have to be made on the side of clarity where meanings are more subtle and ambiguous in the Hebrew.

This richly associative way of writing may help to explain why it has taken so long for a volume of Gilboa's work to appear in English. He has been recognized as a major poet in his own country for more than two decades, winning most of the literary prizes, including the Prime Minister's Award for Creative Writing in 1969 and the Bialik Prize in 1971.

The first poems in the present volume are taken from *Blue and Red*, published in 1963, which is a collection of three earlier books covering a span of almost twenty years. One of the recognizable characteristics of Gilboa's poetry in this early work is his use of the child's point of view. Sometimes a child speaks directly, as in "Isaac" or "Moses." Sometimes the poet evokes his own childhood through memory, as in "A Red Coral." Sometimes he writes as a man who accepts and listens to the child inside him, or changes roles as he discovers that only for a little boy is happiness without end ("Happiness").

However, in the succeeding volumes, if the child is there at all, he is kept at a distance. There was a long silence between the poems collected in *Blue and Red* and *The Lips of Those Asleep*, and it is clear that the existential *angst* spreading to Israel from Europe, together with the succession of wars in the brief history of the renewed State, have made it difficult for Gilboa to recover "the light." Since his joyful tossing of the hundred hats he has been reminded at regular intervals of the price his generation is having to pay for all its achievements. And with these reminders, his personal loss in the Holocaust—his family to which *Red and Blue* is dedicated—is harder to bear.

The first poem in his book *The Lips of Those Asleep*, which appeared in 1968, faces what has been lost—"I forgot whose glory would not fail"—and reminds him of it, "...like recognition burning." Is it better to wake to forgetfulness or to "seize the end of a dream," whatever the dangers? He is still struggling with the nightmare of "Isaac." But set against that now, in some of the poems in this collection, is the dream of Jerusalem, restored and reunited.

"Right now I've no answers," Gilboa says in one poem, yet in the next breath, he adds, "Guard the beautiful, My God, let it be beautiful/that finally is all for now" ("What For").

To be awake is to forget and even to refuse the nightmare memories and therefore to affirm the miracle of life, but it is not easy. When the rain makes everyone run for shelter or, as the children do, for the sheer joy of running, the poet stands at his window watching, and experiences an agonizing paralysis and loss of sensation. A great chasm has opened before him:

> they will suck me into the abyss
> if I step forward if I forget
> and try to step only
> once forward.
>
> ("And All This?")

There are times when nature still puts him in touch with faith, with the sources of his creativity, with the hope that men can continue to communicate with each other and not be overcome by their memories of loss. But even when nature seems to indicate the possibility of growth and change, the awareness of mortality brings sorrow. Gilboa's childlike sense of wonder, so evident in the early poems, may temper this sorrow, but as in the poem "I Know I Won't Come This Way Again," the sorrow remains:

> I know I won't come this way again. Now
> I'll press the palm of my hand on the tree's bark. Maybe
> someone else will come here before it rains and press
> his palm on the bark and unknowing
> add one touch of air to another.
>
> Then the rain will come. All the touching will glide
>                      down with it
> to the base of the tree and sink reaching down to the roots
>                      and rise
> in the trunk and the branches to fill the leaves with new
> greenness. Where will I be when the green and short breath
> of my hands and the one who comes after me join in a flow
> of breathing eternally green.

With the acceptance of his mortality in these poems, comes an increasing sense of isolation. There cannot be enough time, there cannot be enough power or force to sustain life. The poems are very personal, but at the same time, they reflect a mood in Israel, one that became noticeable after the Yom Kippur war. Since all these poems were written before that, they seem prophetic.

We find this anguish in Gilboa even as early as "The Kingdom of Silence" (1952). And twenty years later in "Suddenly with Force:"

> Suddenly with force comes the absence of force.
> Ah the absence of force is dryness.
> Suddenly with force
> like the first rain,
> with the force of the first rain
> comes the drought.
> and with it, not with it, but
> frightening in its aloneness, comes,
> does not come, nothingness does not come, nothingness
> is.

Only when he addresses Jerusalem does he recapture the light:

> Look, here comes the night that is day and not night
> and the endless day comes in the midst of the night.
>                      And it will never darken
> And morning light glows. I wake. Look, here before me,
>                      Jerusalem...
>
>         ("I Knew in the Dream")

Gilboa's most experimental and innovative writing to date is found in the poem cycle *Gazelle, I'll Send You*, published in 1972, from which "Suddenly with Force" is quoted. Who is this gazelle—this fragile being, this prayer, this poet or muse, this alter ego—who bleeds at dawn? In Genesis 49:21, gazelle, *ayala,* is an emblem of Naphtali, one of the sons of Jacob: "a gazelle let loose. He giveth goodly words."

In *Gazelle, I'll Send You,* Gilboa's sense of isolation and fear of death—

> frightened I run and keep running
> treading in place my voice hides
> in my throat between water and water...
>
> ("I Looked Outside")

—continue to alternate with earlier themes of renewal through nature, but the nightmares are more obsessive now:

> ...you suddenly remember a face you know, strange
> but still known, from a distance, that you saw in the dream
> pouring blood from wounds dead now, wallowing in filth
> and the white of its flesh made the earth fade.
>
> ("The Time of Waking")

There are more broken, unfinished lines. A way of coping may be the deliberate confusion of night and day, dreams and reality: "something/strange happened in real life I saw an illusion."

There are many poems of disorientation here. One such is "In the Haze the Sun," in which the sun becomes a ball which can fall to earth and smash "like a great china world." This sun-ball and the ball a child has, perhaps, thrown into the air seem now to coexist, now to replace each other, until it is uncertain who is the dreamer, poet or child. In a nearly hallucinatory state, the poet asks:

> What do I forget, words, their very nature?
> Is it their nature that grew apart from me, estranged,
>                                       no longer mine?
>
> ("What Do I Forget")

Whereas in the earlier poem "Isaac," the child dreams himself out of the original story of Abraham into the Nazi forest, and the poet wakes up with his own hand "drained of blood," in this later collection, in "Standing on Tiptoe," he hangs on to "a shred of a dream":

> Standing on tiptoe shutting my eyes so I won't see what's
> going on in the yard
> on the other side of the fence I know what bewitches me
> there
> it's not because I can't touch it that I close my eyes
> but just to hang on to a shred of a dream
> its wholeness outside my eyelids.
>
> Even in the thick of night when open-eyed I feel a
> curtain of darkness.
>
> Even when the eye is open and looks like cold glittering
> glass.

Gilboa's poetry, thus, has moved from a world where faith was no alien thing ("May the name of the One who brings bread from the sky/be blessed unbridled forever" and "Oh Lord, how close we've been!") to a world so bereft of divinity or the will to choose between good and evil that "nothingness" alone exists. Where is Moses now as he stands on the edge of an abyss? And where is the childlike wonder of "If I Had a Hundred Hats"?

In his introduction to T. Carmi and Dan Pagis: *Selected Poems* (Penguin Books, 1976), M.L. Rosenthal writes, "An ultimately humanistic and even romantic affirmation is implicit in Israeli thought and life." And this may be what finally rescues Gilboa from the despair which threatens to overwhelm him. For with all the distress contained in the *Gazelle* poems, he can still dream that the dead will rise from their graves, and their wounds will not be "pouring blood":

> ...I know I see them
> rising and turning each man to his home...
>
> ("They Will All Rise")

and he still puts into words his yearning to

> ...walk, a man in the garden before the expulsion,
> and hear in the voice of God walking concurrent music

and not a complaint. And God to keep constantly
calling...

("A Bouquet—To Scatter Its Flowers")

Even in fear and in isolation, Gilboa never loses sight of the actual world:

All the time to sit here and look through the window.
Truly the whole world will pass before me in this window.
But I have to pass through the whole world
and put it in this window the whole world.

("All the Time to Sit Here")

In his most recent work, not yet collected in a book, Amir Gilboa re-emphasizes his identification with his people—in poems which are perhaps more apocalyptic than prophetic. He borrows phrases from a wide range of Hebrew literature—from Genesis and Jeremiah and even from himself—in the first poem of *The Lips of Those Asleep,* it is "recognition burning." The dream has turned into nightmare again—his knees "don't support him anymore... he can hardly breathe"—but even in the worst nightmare, Gilboa can see:

...the source of the sunrise
when it burns again, scarlet, as though you'd been seeing it
thousands of years. A thousand years more and its light
will strike your heart and its light will strike your face
till you weep to see your sins white as snow again
and you'll rise up and live.

Shirley Kaufman<br>
Jerusalem, 1979

# THE LIGHT OF LOST SUNS

# I

from *Blue and Red, Collected Poems*
1946 - 1963

**Song of Blue and Red**


As if you walked in snow. And you walked in snow.
Bears came after you. Papa. Mama. Baby.
And you ran as hard as you could. You thought—now I'm
                                                    falling.
And every minute the fear of ten thousand years.

And here you are. Years have passed. Passed.
The beautiful bears are gone. Gone. Will they come back?
Tonight in our garden the pine branches are broken.
And the trees shed tears and blood.

That's the way it is. We are young.
We remember a thousand years.
Look, all the figures will line up at your window
in a row. None are far off. None are near.

**Birth**

The rain is over.

Still it sings in my ears
from the roofs and the trees.
And covers my head
with a blue veil.

Well done, my Lord,
the child is caught in your net.
Now I'll put leaf against leaf
to see how leaf covers leaf
and the raindrops connect.
And I'll call swallows
to the wedding from my heaven,
I'll crown all my windows with flower-pots.

Well done, my Lord,
the child is caught in your net.
I open my eyes,
my land's very wide
and all of it
one flower stem
and green!

Oh Lord, how close we've been!

**In the Dark**

I stretched my hands out into the dark
and the fingers searched for light
trembling with fear of uncertainty.

So I drew the fingers
in toward the palm
and they began to nuzzle
like pups at the teats of a bitch;
there was no end to their safety
in the fold of the clenched fist.

Afterwards, the dawn.

**Isaac**

Early in the morning the sun took a walk in the woods
with me and my father
my right hand in his left.

A knife flashed between the trees like lightning.
And I'm so scared of the fear in my eyes facing blood
                                                        on the leaves.
Father father come quick and save Isaac
so no one will be missing at lunchtime.

It's I who am butchered, my son,
my blood's already on the leaves.
And father's voice was choked.
And his face pale.

I wanted to cry out, struggling not to believe,
I tore my eyes open
and woke.

And my right hand was drained of blood

**Moses**

I went up to Moses and said to him:
Arrange the troops like this...
He looked at me and he
arranged them as I said.

And who did not see me then so honored!
There was Sarah from my childhood
in whose name I planned to build a town.
There was the one with long legs from the girls' farm.
There was Malvina from Rabat in Malta.
Dina from the Italian-Yugoslav border.
And Riyah from the northern lowland.

And very proud I rushed to Moses
to show him exactly where...
But suddenly I realized
that the one most
carved and sealed in my name
wasn't there.

Moses, Moses, you lead the people.
Look, I'm so tired, I want to sleep some more,
I'm still a child.

## All Ordinary Things

All ordinary things wait for the calm rising anxious and slow from people whose lives were spent in a blazing storm.

All ordinary things are very patient, their appearance takes on a sad grandeur as twilight falls with the gold day at the feet of the wanderer alone on an empty plain. And they are so beautiful you forget everything. It's like spring in the heart of a boy sitting on the bank of a lake. And all the bells ringing around you pouring out stream after stream though you can't see stone towers or turrets anywhere.

All ordinary things lie safe and dreamy like flocks of sheep. Like biblical wells on ancient crossroads. Like eternal walls where gods were revealed on both sides when lightning lit their antiquity when rain rinsed their gray faces generation after generation. That also remember their sorrow when the first rain caused nothing to grow on their backs.

All ordinary things keep stroking consoling hands hidden inside and sounds of silence that soothe the eyes the forehead the face of a man weathered by time, come back from the heart of the storm.

And the ordinary things put him together and cover him with God whispering all the secrets of his thirst in voices overflowing from the depths.

## Everywhere

I passed a tree and it seemed as though it passed me
and I was so touched I put my trust in it.
And I was so glad I didn't know what to call it
and I didn't know if my father sent it to me or my brother.

Either way I rejoiced in it fully
and hugged it in front of the houses and the whole street.
Now my lips shove through the skin to the warmth of its blood
and it keeps its breath from my embrace—
and stuck to the nape of my neck are the eyes
of the memory of my father and brother *from beyond the street.*

The blessed! They are everywhere. Every day they are here.
I'm given only a second to hug them. Sometimes. So near.

## A Red Coral

Do you remember the mulberry tree, how the young leaves
                              stroked us with bright green
and its fruit bewitched us like a flash of great passion—
blood too ripe to contain dripped on the meadows with
                                         each mulberry.
A hiding-place? Ah! How our hearts rejoiced
to find it when first desired, before it grew high
with laughing that showed our revolt.

Oh how we little ones walked on paths of an early Friday
with silver gray scales in our eyes from the fish in the river
where we never fished—
or maybe you too can't remember now
if the village girls came back
from harvest or windmill. And how
we blushed as they laughed when they slid down to bathe
their full breasts, so full,
so white.

And how our eyes lit up at the first gypsy's cry—
as he burst between stalks of wheat
as out of a womb—
and thistles and thornflowers reeked with the fragrance
                                         of spikenard.
Little gypsies all over dipping their bread in salt,
a colt whinnied into his oats
tossing everything gold around him
in arcs of chaff.

What a sight! May the name of the One who brings bread
                                               from the sky
be blessed unbridled forever.

Afterwards I think someone blew on a horn
and it wasn't evening. Oh, how very late the evening came.
How good are the tents! The thorns of nettles put out
                                        the scorching flames
and gave a new mother a shelter of shade.

## Happiness

Everyone in the street asked How come you're so happy,
and being happy, I didn't hear
until I almost got to the end of the street.
There was a little boy playing in the sand at the end
$$\text{of the street.}$$
I said to him Come on and be happy too.
He said to me You're at the end of the street.

Everyone in the street asked How come you're so happy,
and being happy, I didn't hear
until I almost got to the end of the happiness.
I was a little boy who doesn't reach the end of happiness.
I said to myself you'll be more and more happy
and you'll never reach the end of happiness.

Everyone in the street asked How come you're so happy,
and being happy, I didn't hear.
And anyway I don't hear when I'm happy.
There was a long day when I wasn't happy,
and I wondered why everyone asked about my happiness then.
And sorrow as big as the happiness ate at my heart.

**If I Had a Hundred Hats**


If I had a hundred hats on my head
a hundred hats      a hundred colors
a hundred hats      a hundred colors and shades of colors
a hundred hats      a rain of colors

if I had a hundred hats on my head
I'd go into the market place
clear me a way to the market place
and toss them in happiness

if I had a hundred hats on my head
I'd go into the market place
and everybody would clear me a way
and wait for my waving the hats

if I had a hundred hats on my head
a hundred hats      a hundred colors and shades of colors
if I had a hundred hats      and a high sun going
straight to my head      straight to my colors

oh the crowd      ready to shout its cry of praise
its great heart thumping in the square
heart of the crowd waiting

for the waving of a hundred hats      a hundred
                                          colors and shades

## Our Eyes Closing

Brightness in the morning. Blue in the trough.
And a fine thread oils the water covered with seaweed.
Seaweed. And sting. Without sting. Nothing.
And it's good to rest like this on a plain bench
in a corner of a desolate garden.
And be quiet. Quiet. And hear the story of the wind
the wind carried and wafted over our heads,
and only the dust only the dust tossed in our eyes.
Eyes. Our eyes. And all this has passed.
Passed. Gone. Or perhaps gone aside to rest. To rest
in front of our eyes closing

there.
There on the top of the tree
they redden. Small laugh. Smile in a poem. Trace of a dream
                                                        while awake—
an apple.

And still the wind

**Song All Day Long**


Sir, I've walked all day to see your face.
Fierce winds beat against my face and knees,
fierce winds blocked my steps,
fierce winds dimmed the lamps of my eyes.

Sir, I've walked all day to see your face.
Your strength kept me going: with every step I whispered

                                          your name.

With every step I sealed your name
in rock, in mud, in sand.
From stem to stem.
From pillar to pillar.
I knew I would see you alive.
You wouldn't die.
You wouldn't die.
Not you—
the chief of the tribe.

Sir, I've walked all day to see your face
and I find you a slave.

# The Kingdom of Silence

Cries still stray in the field
and the high priest gives thanks
for the victory. Heaps of ashes
announce: a summer of blood has burned out.
Its embers already smoke in the book.
Silence seeps in. At twilight
the crowd's voices blur.
Silence. The falling
of leaves. Soon autumn.

And distant. Everything distant. Everything
seemingly calm. The rain will fall again
on smoking chimneys. And suddenly
a storm will rage in the rivers.

Winter. A fisherman mends his net.
Spring will come. Water will rise
and subside. A willow will bend
its branches from the banks. In gardens
the trees will blossom. Young eyes seek
love on the beach.
And the view takes a thousand forms
in the eyes of a thousand as one.
Summer will blaze where they lie.
One moment drunk and the next confronted
with fire. Called to battle.
Strong echoes answer the voices

that cry. The slayers and slain.
Great mountains will stab
through their eyesockets. Flames
will glut on them. Will stretch tongues. Will glut
on their tongues as they lick the dust. And flames
will be ashes. Scrolls
among pages smoking
will extoll the kingdom of silence. Sleepers
will extoll the kingdom of silence. The low
brought lower in fragments of weeping.
The lost will bang on tin cups.
The tin will rattle. Autumn
will drop its leaves
in the fields. In the roads. Everything
bound up in books will rest. *Selah*. Each generation
will rest. *Selah*. Embers
part blind
are silent
silent
the legions.

And there's no one to come. And no one
to flee. No longer a voice
bequeathed by the dead. Just one who goes on.

## Joshua's Face

And Joshua looks down on my face. And his face
is hammered gold. A dream embalmed. And cold.
And at my feet the sea strikes endless time.
I'm sick of its wailing. Perhaps, about to die.
But I am forced to stay alive
forever.
My brother's face rises in a cloud
to read my footsteps in the sea-washed sand.

The sea strikes and withdraws. Strikes and withdraws.
The wars of nature conditioned by laws.
Myself in the wind. Different. Running far.
Now Joshua also rests from war
and leaves his people a home
though he carved no tomb of his own
in the mountains of Ephraim.
Night after night
he walks the sky.
And I am sick, perhaps, about to die
barefoot in cold moon sand
on the shore
while the end roars in me, a roar
that strikes my own death at my feet
wave after wave—

high over many lives
may he be raised and glorified.

**Samson**

And Samson gets old
and sleepless at night.
As a child he had raised the world on its axis with one hand.
As a young man he wanted to die on the night of his
                                    seventeenth birthday.

He didn't want to die old; seventeen and a day.
That's why he fastened torches to the tails of three
                                    hundred foxes
to burn everything.
In his twenties he meant to do wonders till the day of his death
                                    at thirty-three

When they gouged out his eyes
he prayed that he'd still see his daughters' weddings.
At eighty he's not really grown
and mixed-up in time, he dreams like a child just born.

While the gates of his Gaza sleep in their power.

And Delilah

## In Very Ancient Days

In very ancient days
everything was sun
and everything was mountain
with the valley in the mountain's hollow
and everything was valley
with the mountain in its lap.

And when the great distant gods
seeded the universe so it would give birth
distant stars in the sky saw
a legend born into sadness
and their faces grew dark
and their eyes full of tears

and the rain began to rain

## II

from *The Lips of Those Asleep*
1966-1968

**With Force I'll Seize the End of a Dream**


With force I'll seize the end of a dream.
It's not allowed to cross the lips.
Nor even grow in memory
lest we be stricken.
Oh Jerusalem.

In the dense thicket of sleep
I forgot whose glory would not fail.
I had always known it. Like recognition burning.
Until I woke one day as if after seventy years.

And we can't make words for the lips of those asleep.
Years will fill every cup with a curse.
On a table, a glass of smoky dreams.
Soon, God help my eyes, I won't
see it.

**Every Time I Discover a New America**

Every time I discover a new America
and travel in it and look around. And it's a good thing
                                                       I don't hang
it on a wall. Mostly. Very mostly. Because after
a while I see it already exists. Already
has been. Will be.

But I'm very lucky. Even the America
no one has yet discovered
that appears to me different from time to time. Even
that America. The many. America
multiplied. I don't admit it even to myself. Don't
keep it even to myself. I let it go.

And with it me too.

**What For**

What for, one might ask, and I'd have no answer, though
maybe I would. Many trains have passed me and I didn't
ask where to so I wouldn't know where from. Airplanes
    have circled without
stopping, without coming down, without landing. My
    beautiful girl moved
as if in a photograph without changing, except
    with the rays of the sun
which lean toward the dark and so keep on moving. Like poems
which are born and which aren't.
What for, if one asked I'd have no answer, though
I know what's way off in the past and the future. But right now
    I've no
answers. Guard the beautiful, my God, let it be beautiful.
That finally is all for now.

**And All This?**


And all this? And from here I'll see
distant craters beyond me where
suns were shattered distant craters
oiled by the light of lost suns
and all this and nothing else
from the distant craters to where I am and everything
as it was before living creatures to where I am now and onwards
again a new emptiness
endless except that the pits don't yet
smolder they will suck me into the abyss
if I step forward if I forget
and try to step only
once forward.

# I Go on Disappearing from Myself


I go on disappearing from myself and suddenly I see
myself walking ahead of me. If only I could cry.
No smiles no tears. Sad enough for tears. And I whisper to
myself oh my brother my brother. And my brother goes ahead
of me and bears
my face. His eyes in my eyes. And my being
in my non-being. And where shall we go. And we are over
a great abyss.

**Now Seeing There's Rain**

Now seeing there's rain I look through the window and
                                                                 see every-
one running. Now seeing there's rain I'll go out in the rain to
see if it chases me too but maybe I shouldn't go out maybe I
shouldn't know since my hands won't move and my feet
                                                                       just walk
for the sake of walking maybe I shouldn't know that the rain
falls for nothing and it's separate and I'm separate only clothes
on my skin and I shouldn't get them wet again.

**Those Were the Last Dances**


Those were the last dances. Now I
know that I moved in a mask others put
on my face, not me. I got there late
they were already in place. The light was dim.
And the eyes were veiled in a kind of not wanting,
                                              wanting to perform
as they should at these parties when all of us
were angels on nights of other days. Now I
know that those were the last dances and that
was the best time I've ever had
God help us all when I got there late
they were all in their places and I thought it's all
the same. Now that it's already tomorrow I know I was
late but I'll never forget the last dances.

There were never any first dances.

## Those Who Know What's in Heaven

Those who know what's in heaven do not tell
they only dream visions and hear words
in the deep cellars they carry with them
and when they go out among people they are not noticed
only the blind ask them for help crossing the road
and the deaf long to read the right time from their lips
on the other hand the children don't want or ask anything
                                                from them
but look into and after them and dream visions
and hear words and the rest of their lives
recall a miracle they never tell

and always want to tell.

**I Know I Won't Come this Way Again**


I know I won't come this way again. Now
I'll press the palm of my hand on the tree's bark. Maybe
someone else will come here before it rains and press
his palm on the bark and unknowing
add one touch of air to another.

Then the rain will come. And all the touching will glide
                                                down with it
to the base of the tree and sink reaching down to the roots
                                                            and rise
in the trunk and the branches to fill the leaves with new
greenness. Where will I be when the green and short breath
of my hands and the one who comes after me join in a flow
of breathing eternally green.

## To Jerusalem My City

1.

To Jerusalem my city I wanted to say aloud
words that I whisper to her heart
so my ears too would hear what my heart feels

2.

To catch all the strands of the web still floating in a straight
line in the air and to make them one again

so that a heart beat would pulse from one end to the other
                                                                                                   in endless
perfect frequency

and the circuit would renew itself forever humming my speech
with all the words I know and don't know

beyond all the tongues I've seen in the mirror in rainbow colors
from bottom to top

and more

3.

I knew in the dream the dream wouldn't fly like a dream.
I knew in the dream that in me myriads are dreaming
                                                                                                    the dream.

I woke. Midnight. Who turns the dark of night into the
                                            light of day?
The sun stands still in the window in the dream as on that day
                                            in Gibeon I recall.
Look, here comes the night that is day and not night
and the endless day comes in the midst of night. And it will
                                            never darken.
And morning light glows. I wake. Look, here before me,
                                            Jerusalem.
And I see it. I see it with myriads of eyes.
Was there ever anything like this
a dream dreamed at the same time
by myriads while they dream.

# III

from *Gazelle, I'll Send You*
1971-1972

**Gazelle, I'll Send You**


Gazelle, I'll send you to the wolves they are not in the forest
even in town on the sidewalks you'll flee from them
                                         your terrified
eyes are beautiful they will envy me seeing how you flow-
er frightened and your soul

I'll send you into the thick of the
battle it's no longer for me

my heart gazelle watching you bleed at dawn

### The Whole Land Is Mine

The whole land is mine asleep and awake I see
one long dream electric spirits making
flocks of swallows hover in branches of the tree weaving
                                                                              the window
and my bones and flesh in a dizzy wind over a huge land
all mine.

**They Will All Rise**


They will all rise. I know I see them
rising and turning each man to his home, each to his home
seeing the road they remember
and a split second wipes out the distance and binds
distance to distance in a wonder of dream whether
dreamed or not. And meanwhile
his wife already laughs through the tears and his children
rub their cheeks on his cheek, telling the story
he waited to hear again whispered
in mouths of the roots of plants

**I Looked Outside**

I looked outside. Pools of water.
Strips of silt between each pool
sprouting with stems of hands
their voices unheard
fish were tossed on the shore
from the water their eyes behind
on the water still watching me
frightened I run and keep running
treading in place my voice hides
in my throat between water and water

**Far Far Outside**


Far far outside, behind the wall,
lips bubble great words
unbroken unweaned to the street.
And a sea in the intervals, eyelids fluttering,
now rain after midnight,
above and below, in the heart of the world,
prays

## To Pluck Stars

To pluck stars, berries from a bush at night
out of the dark, the velvet, time for the one set apart
breathing sweetly, wrapped warm in
kind loneliness, leaving commotion,
voiced by the silence, ripening with a secret.
And to go further, as if on the paws of a cat
knowing the ease of immortality that steals a portion of life
not divided, a godly emergency ration
between being and being, between nothing and nothing,
and to lie bundled up on the ground, smelling the earth
that good crust of bread, growing and growing
an embryo in the belly of some great mercy.

## The Time of Waking

The time of waking from death from the dream
to a nagging ache, insistent, depressing,
which passes at last to return
and show up like the seasons, foreseen like the seasons,
dangling before your eyes like a threatening finger
                                                      between times
intermittent, not forgotten. But the time of waking from death
from the dream as if everything's blank for an instant
when suddenly washing your body and face as if cleansing
your soul, you suddenly remember a face you know, strange
but still known, from a distance, that you saw in the dream
pouring blood from wounds dead now, wallowing in filth
and the white of its flesh made the earth fade

## A Patch of the Sea

A patch of the sea, flesh, to swim in it,
in marble, in alabaster, which will grow hot and finally melt,
also the eyes, will first become blue, will wake up again
to a patch of the sea, to equate blue with blue
in a cave of the sea, secrets of far-away days
which the sun will turn gold, last rays from the hiding of
                                                                                    sorrow,
beauty that's saved for eyes which no longer
look except toward the west

**In the Haze the Sun**

In the haze the sun an orange ball, smooth
as if thrown in the air, at the cry of a child might
begin the trip back, increasing and gathering speed,
if it falls nearby it will smash, he'll see
thousands and thousands of splinters like a great
china world, and the world will go on like this without
moving without a polished ball until it will clear again
the sun will move again will stay up high again
a ball in its glory and this time he won't see it eye to eye
because a child won't see anything but a ball thrown
in the air in the dream in the day

**See an Unwalled City**


See an unwalled city by day a wasteland
whitens distance coming toward you
at night from every side legions rise and
rise upon you
an unwalled city by day your name
swells without limit
at night you contract and contract
and your name grows small within you

**What Peace for His Soul**

What peace for his soul if his tracks in the water,
where everything is erased, disappear after he passes
and the magic of his castles drowns with him
a couch for dreams if they come
with eternal winter, cold loneliness, blue-eyed steel freezes
in the forgetting of an eternal abyss.

## My Secret, Mine, Sees My Face

My secret, mine, sees my face among roses,
in clear water on a forgotten morning in a mountain forest
my secret, mine, comes to me from the distance, from then,
                                                                               suddenly
when I walk in a worn-out street as it warms
seeing, suddenly, for an instant, my face among roses,
blushing like them with shame.

Passing. Quickly. Onward. Only the memory.
An instant.

**Its Leaves Seen**


Its leaves seen as for the last time heads drooping,
the pale white turns gray growing frail,
hard for them to remember the joy of budding, festival
                              of bloom,
fragrance drenching a piece of land,
and no point in trying to recall its memory,
its season passed, as if it hadn't been
before spring comes new,
if it comes, its fragrance with it,

and already, of course, another

**Squeezed in a Bus**

Squeezed in a bus suddenly my back is palpable
nightmares wall of a body cold fat flesh ancient locked prison
shoves between me and the good metal back to cling to.

A life that's almost closed-in I didn't remember a nightmare
wall of this fat cold flesh
and here squeezed in a bus when I try
to lean on this good metal back.
And this loathing.

And the hatred rising in me.

## Standing on Tiptoe

Standing on tiptoe shutting my eyes so I won't see
                              what's going on in the yard
on the other side of the fence I know what bewitches me there
it's not because I can't touch it that I close my eyes
but just to hang on to a shred of a dream
its wholeness outside my eyelids.

Even in the thick of night when open-eyed I feel a
                                       curtain of darkness.

Even when the eye is open and looks like cold glittering glass.

## And on the Great Waters

And on the great waters when I
seem to have opened, or else they were opened, the dams
                                            and the waters spilled
and the waters ran out revealing a hollowed land of silt
                                                               of nothing
cradle of nothing, not to be measured, not to contain all these
                                                          primordial eons
where God alone casts His shadow
and a fierce cold
and suddenly dogs chase after dogs

and life barks
in a cradle of nothing I dream

## Finally I Go to the Man Who Set Traps

Finally I go to the man who set traps for the birds
ask his pardon, for trying to stop his playing with the lives
                                                    of others,
curse my folly, for why should I take the joy from the drive
he was careful to keep at a high pitch all the time,
especially when the birds have already flown off and it seems
they twitter and chirp to me way up over my head.
And they're sure I also have traps my hands are traps,
and they'll never land in my palms stretched toward them.

### How Would I Stand Then

How would I stand then, what side of my face expose
                                               to the light,
to people who pass, and how would I act if suddenly
a cat crossed my path, would I be cool, smiling, and people
would see, and I'd keep on going, or would I hide
my eyes and people not see me, and would I switch
my direction, and if the sun blazed hard
would I lean on the wall or drag a trail of shadow after me
to cool the sweaty, red-faced shame when there is no shadow
and would I still care about people who don't see me at all,
who don't exist at all, even though I carry them with me.

## All the Time to Sit Here

All the time to sit here and look through this window.
Truly the whole world will pass before me in this window.
But I have to pass through the whole world
and put it in this window the whole world.

## How They Run into the Day

How they run into the day!
Into what do they run? They're already within.
Perhaps into the sea. But even that at the end
will bring them to day. Day is land.
And sea joins day to a day.
You can't get away from the land.

**Suddenly with Force**

Suddenly with force comes the absence of force.
Ah the absence of force is dryness.
Suddenly with force
like the first rain,
with the force of the first rain
comes the drought.
And with it, not with it, but
frightening in its aloneness, comes,
does not come, nothingness does not come, nothingness
is.

## A Bouquet—To Scatter Its Flowers

A bouquet—to scatter its flowers on the floor and the table
not as a bunch bound tight and thrust in a vase like a finger of
                                                              menacing beauty,
gardens and orchards—to raise them between closed walls,
and walk, a man in the garden before the expulsion,
and hear in the voice of God walking concurrent music
and not a complaint. And God to keep constantly
calling. A voice walking
let it walk

## If in Pain a Light Feather

If in pain a light feather what will you say
it will fly if they throw it to the ground
if the wind tosses it to every wind
it will sink touching not touching the earth
from above what will you say
the whole weight of the earth below it holds
earth a light feather
every wind will toss it to every wind
what will you say

**What Do I Forget**

What do I forget, words, their very nature?
Is it their nature that grew apart from me, estranged,
                                        no longer mine?
Where does my house stand now, and if I build it
what materials have been collected, and where.
I got up late, some webs, there or not there,
tangled me in a dream, was it from sweet laziness
I did not want to untie myself?
No, all the materials, opal agate amethyst,
begged me to put them in basement and roof
and a glittering crown was already in reach to set
on the top, a splendid building, and this
wrong calculation of a tiny flick
made everything collapse and found me awake
sprawled among ruins.
What was it I forgot, the spell of words, their very nature
to wreck and I, yes, only in a dream, was ready
not ready to build.

## I'm Certain I Went

I'm certain I went, out of an illusion, to look
for my footprints on a road that was covered with buildings and
                                          bordered with fences
ages ago the signs that I left were erased and even then
I knew that I wouldn't remember them something strange
                                            happened
I saw my footprints clearly engraved even
in the walls of houses the lattice of fences all
the signs shining in the dark as if anointed
phosphorous cats' eyes in the dark I walked
by their light I passed through the fences I crossed
the walls as if they were never there were
only those days in which I left signs
and I knew then I wouldn't remember them and something
strange happened in real life I saw an illusion

## To Move on Slowly Slowly

To move on slowly slowly. Not go.

To go, subduing distance step by step by step before you.
To move on, erasing step after step after step behind you,
and to come to her room cleansed of everything free of every-
                        thing born to what's left of your being
gasping, reviving courage gathering material to knead your
                                                      offspring
to plant in them your made-up world before you leave
toward what.

From need, it seems, and the circumstances of the
                                          present situation
you know
that you ought to
move on slowly slowly. Not go.

**Look at this Man**


Look at this man who crosses here on the bridge
and what is in front of him is the water under him
now he flows with the water far away far away

look at this man who crosses on the bridge
I know truly his heart is like mine
now his heart flows with the water
toward another country
toward another loneliness

river of my heart, wait for me
I finish my prayer and run, maybe

# IV
from *Recognition Burning*
1974

**If You Get up and Leave**


If you get up and leave your country
and your homeland you will not leave even if you go far
the migration of birds will bring painful greetings
from a burning summer in a winter wasted and eaten
                                        by whiteness
and your longing will stretch over distance joined
by a steel thread strong and unseen
that butchers the flesh and pours in the soul sweet poisons
of vintage wine spilled with sorrow
on a land of poison hemlock. And it will be like wormwood
in your mouth only a last memory left to recover
an old taste bestowed on you but withheld
from your sons and whether they greet you
in the ancient language or in the new
both will be sickening to your ears
because you will hear it in a strange foreign country.

## He'll Take You with Him

He'll take you with him far away and there
under the willows you'll weep on knees
that don't support him any more. He can hardly breathe.
And from the weeping that keeps rising and falling
like verses from Lamentations
your pleasant son Ephraim will be born again to walk
in the mountains of his greenness. You will want
to imagine how he looks
but you'll have to be patient who knows
how many thousands of years before a dream will grow again
from the waste and desolation of the dwellings you left.
And everything you plowed will be covered by ruins
and the one who kept silent will raise you again
                                                  from the plunder
to go toward the source of the sunrise
when it burns again, scarlet, as though you'd been seeing it
thousands of years. A thousand years more and its light
will strike your heart and its light will strike your face
till you weep to see your sins white as snow again
and you'll rise up and live